*From
Spring
to
Spring*

From Spring to Spring

POEMS AND PHOTOGRAPHS

By

Lois Duncan

The Westminster Press

PHILADELPHIA

Book Design by Dorothy Alden Smith

First edition

Published by The Westminster Press ®
Philadelphia, Pennsylvania

PRINTED IN THE UNITED STATES OF AMERICA

9 8 7 6 5 4 3 2 1

Library of Congress Cataloging in Publication Data

Duncan, Lois, 1934–
   From spring to spring.

   Includes index.
   SUMMARY: Presents a collection of poems on a variety
of topics throughout the seasons, many with a religious
flavor.
   1. Children's poetry, American. [1. American poetry]
I. Title.
PS3554.U464F7   1982   811'.54   82–11100
ISBN 0–664–32695–1

*For my photographer father
Joseph Janney Steinmetz
with love*

Contents

Ours Is the World

Ours is the world that God has made,
The wind and water, sun and shade.
We breathe its magic with the air.
Its miracles are everywhere!
A snowball bush, a climbing tree,
The foam that frosts the summer sea,
The family, friends, and pets that give
A meaning to the life we live—
Each plays a special, lovely part
Creating music of the heart.

Throughout the year, from spring to spring,
God writes the songs that children sing.

Flower Song

This was a year when Spring forgot.
She stayed in the southlands far too long.
Snow lay piled on the garden path
And winter winds sang the robin's song.

When God gave her a gentle shove
Spring set things right. In a matter of hours
She changed all the icicles into leaves,
And all the snowballs she turned to flowers.

Bird Song

There was a day, the Bible says,
When God created birds.
We are not told much more than that.
I guess there were no words
That could describe the rushing sound
As they burst into flight,
The billion wings that blocked the sun
And changed the day to night,
The feathered snowstorm in the sky,
The squawks that filled the air—
It must have been impressive, but
I'm glad I wasn't there.

Garden Song

I went into the garden.
The breeze was turning cool.
The flowers all lay napping
Beside a little pool.

Grass was flecked with shadows
And the air was sweet.
I bent to touch the blossoms
Dreaming at my feet.

Touching them, I whispered
A silly little prayer,
Because they were so lovely
And I was happy there.

Like gentle, drowsy children
The sleepy flowers lay.
I told them all my secrets,
And then I went away.

Song for a Good Day

Once in a while there's a day when you wake
And you know that you never can make a mistake.
Your breakfast is all of the things you like most.
The jelly stays put on the top of the toast.
You're late for the school bus—it comes in a minute.
A seat by the window has nobody in it.
You get back a test, and it's marked with a star.
You run in a race. You're the winner by far.
The sun is so bright, and the sky is so blue
That you know God has made them
   especially for you!

Once in a while it can happen that way
On a beautiful, wonderful, very good day.

Dream Song

If God made the world
As I wished it might be,
I would fly through the clouds
And I'd walk on the sea.

There are those who suppose
That I can't do these things,
For my legs are not strong
And I do not have wings.

But life isn't always
The way that it seems,
For I fly in my mind—
And I walk in my dreams.

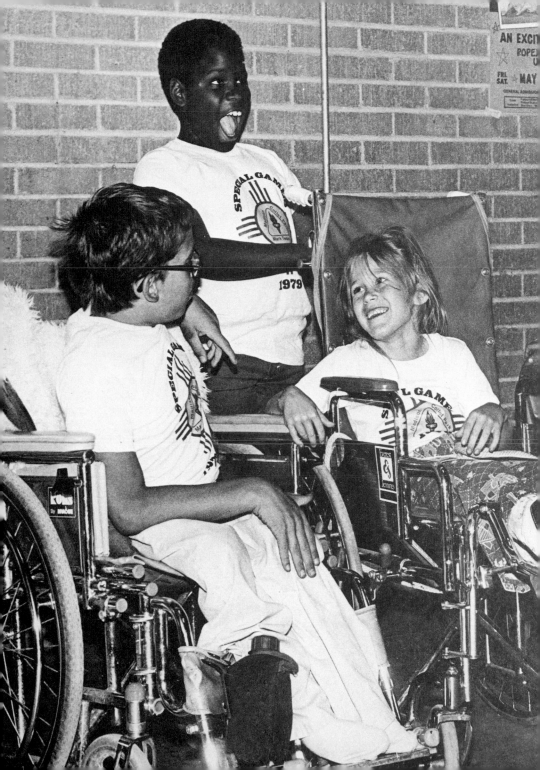

Wedding Song

My aunt was married by the lake
Beneath the rustling trees.
She and her love stood hand in hand.
Their music was the breeze.

Their faces were aglow with joy,
The sun caressed their hair.
Although we were not in a church,
I know that God was there.

Birth Song

Deep in my mother,
Quiet and waiting,
How many months, I
Dwelt in her softness,
Cushioned and gentled,
While I was growing,
While I was waiting
For God to call me,
For God to tell me,
"Now is the moment—"

Then I came shouting
Into the world!

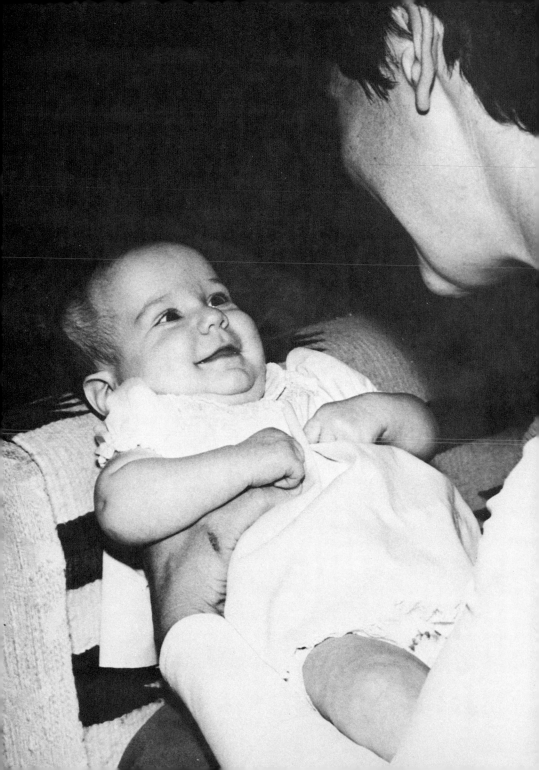

Song of Frustration

I have a sister who writes on walls
And rides her tricycle through the halls
And drowns her dolls in the bathroom sink
And takes the last of the orange drink
And sucks her thumb and screams at bugs
And hides her sandwiches under the rugs
And rips my books and won't take naps
And always sits on the company's laps.

I have a sister who's almost four.
Sometimes I wish that she lived next door.

Song of Triumph

When first I asked Mother
The answer was, "No."
I asked the next morning.
I still couldn't go.

I asked her and asked her.
She said, "You're too small,"
And sometimes she just
Wouldn't answer at all.

I asked her at breakfast,
At lunchtime, and then
At dinner last evening
I asked her again.

Till finally she sighed
And she told me, "All right—"
SO I'M SLEEPING OVER
AT RICKY'S TONIGHT!

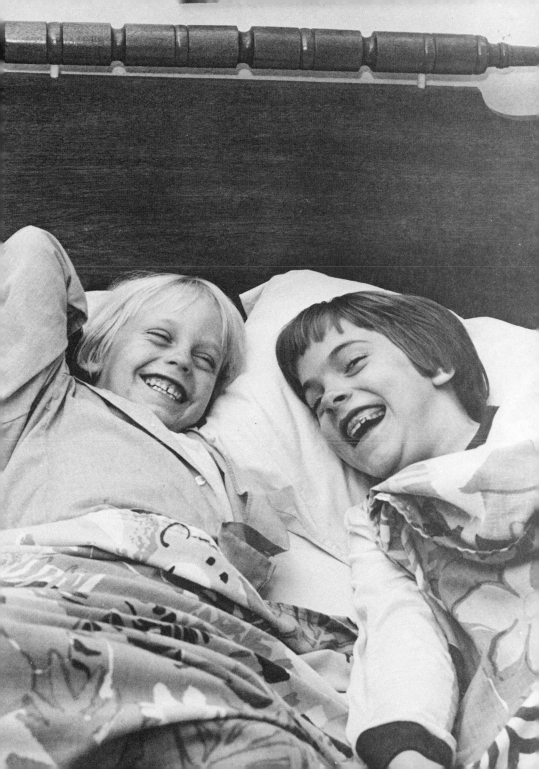

Grandfather Song

Grandfather Days have a special glow.
They move at a pace that is sure and slow
With a different rhythm, a different rhyme,
A blend of today and another time.
A grandfather speaks, and behind his words
Are the winds of spring, or the cry of birds
In the autumn sky, or the sound of rain
Making puddles grow in a country lane.
From a beautiful world that was yesterday,
A grandfather's love comes a long, long way
And wraps you round with a golden haze—
The gentle magic of Grandfather Days.

Song for a Bad Day

This was a day when nothing went right.
My brother and I had a breakfast fight;
I spilled my milk on the kitchen floor
So I couldn't go to the grocery store.
My dress got wet from the garden hose,
I fell on the slide and bruised my toes,
My crayons got lost and the TV broke
And my bicycle had a busted spoke.
This was a day when things went wrong.
Days like that seem to last so long.

Treasure Song

When God gave us summer
The gift brought as well
A storehouse of treasures
Too splendid to sell.
God tossed out a handful
Of sparkling light,
That turned into fireflies
To brighten the night.
God emptied out pockets
And scattered all over
The taste of raspberries,
The scent of wild clover,
The splash of the sun on
The curl of a stream,
And the lilt of a lark
Being waked from a dream.
What marvelous presents
To hand to a child!
When God gave us summer,
I think that he smiled.

Tree Song

Did you ever see a Summertime Tree,
Grand and gracious and green,
With spaces left where the leaves don't meet
So summer can slip between?

Growing and glowing, it covers the sky,
Full and flowing and fine!
Did you ever see a Summertime Tree?
No? Then I'll show you mine.

Song for a Journey

Once on a golden afternoon
We went to find a dream.
We saw a million leaping trout
Swept from a rushing stream;
A monster, crouched among the reeds
Within its shadowed lair;
A mermaid, laughing on a rock,
With seaweed in her hair.

A message in a floating jar,
Five hundred miles from land,
Swept past us, and a pirate chest,
Half buried in the sand,
Proved filled with coins and precious gems
That sparkled in the sun.
We tossed them to a flock of swans
Who ate them one by one.

How many wonders one can find,
What journeys one can take,
All on a golden afternoon
Upon a golden lake!

Mud Song

A stint in the shower
Will get your skin clean,
But it's sort of a bore
If you know what I mean.

A soak in the tub does
Not offer much hope
When you've gotten too old
To play boats with the soap.

A dip in the pool can
Be fun when it's hot,
But your eyes start to hurt
If you swim there a lot.

When God made the world, I
Am glad there was time
To dig holes for puddles
And fill them with slime.

Song of Wealth

Wealth of summer,
Dreamers' gold—
For so short a time
It is mine to hold.
Gold in the meadow,
Gold on the hill,
Slanted light when
The world is still;
Golden currency,
Mine to spend,
Here where the sun-
Warmed grasses bend,
That shining glory
Beyond compare—
The gold of heaven
Upon my hair.

Moon Song

Up and down the silent beach
The silent shadows glide.
The moon leans out across the dunes
To draw the heavy tide.

The ocean sighs against the shore.
Its depths stir restlessly.
What is this globe of silver light
That it controls the sea?

Star Song

The stars above are pale and high
Like pinpricks in a sheet of sky,
And through these holes the gentle light
Of heaven dots the summer night.

The stars below are churning gold,
Too fast to count, too hot to hold.
They leap and flash and flicker out.
I sometimes like to think about

The different sorts of joy they bring—
The stars that smile—the stars that sing.

Song for a Slow Trip

A ride on a turtle
Is terribly slow,
For you never quite know
Where a turtle will go.

Yes, a trip made by turtle
Will take you a while,
But you'll know when it's over
You traveled in style.

Song for a Farm Child

I was born in a land of fields
Where the only seas were seas of grain,
Golden waves in the gentle wind
          And summer rain.

Though I stand on this rocky ledge
And watch the leaping, silver spray
And the flash of gulls before the sun,
          I would not stay.

Splendid and strong is the pounding surf
And the beautiful, endless stretch of sky—
But I was born in a quiet place
          Where blackbirds fly.

Horse Song

Each morning when I go to school
Old Possum waits for me.
She grazes by the school-yard fence
Until at last I'm free.

She never doubts that I will come.
She doesn't count the hours,
Just stands and dreams of sunlit trails
And meadows filled with flowers.

Old Possum's lived a good, long life.
One year, I guess, she'll go
To graze in pastures greener than
The ones earth creatures know.

When I get old, I'll meet her there.
She'll wait a while. She doesn't care.

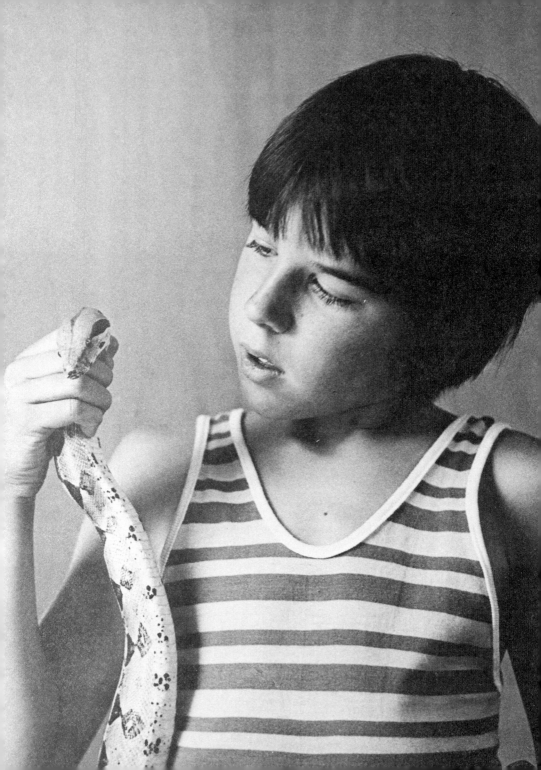

Snake Song

A snake's a strangely fashioned thing,
A strip of hose around a spring,
A coil of wire compressed inside
A cool and dry and scaly hide.

Why is man frightened of its ways?
What is the power in its gaze
That Eve, held captive by its eyes,
Gave up her rights to Paradise?

Song for Little Churches

Magnificent cathedrals
Cry, "Glory to the Lord!"
They offer God the splendor
Their masses can afford.

Their spires are high and regal,
But, scattered through the land,
In villages and hamlets,
The little churches stand.

They nestle on the hillsides,
They dot the fields and plains.
They're chilly in the winter;
They're musty when it rains.

A child born in a stable
Might smile to hear this prayer—
Lord, bless all little churches
And those who worship there.

Phone Song

My parents tell me, when I was two
The only thing I would say was, "Goo."
They'd try to teach me such simple words
As "dog" and "kitty" and "trees" and "birds."
I wouldn't say them. I "gooed" instead
From the time I rose till I went to bed.
I'd "goo" goodnight to my teddy bears,
I'd "goo" to God in my evening prayers;
And later still, when the night grew deep,
I'd "goo-goo" quietly in my sleep.
My parents dreaded the thought that I
Might keep on "gooing" as years went by
And never speak in a normal way.
And then things changed. I said, "Hi" one day.
They tell me now that they should have known
The day would come when I'd find the phone.

Song of Change

Up from the river a wind is blowing,
The wind we longed for the summer through.
The sky which was golden and hot and glowing
Is high above us and strangely blue.

Here, where the apple tree was budding
Ready to bloom, we hear a sound
And turn to find it's an apple thudding
Heavy and hard to the sunbaked ground.

A wind comes whipping up from the river,
Tossing some leaves to the browning lawn.
We look at each other, surprised, and shiver,
And suddenly—swiftly—summer is gone.

Balloon Song

Balloons, balloons, and more balloons!
A hundred different colored moons!
Bright balls as far as one can see—
They make the sky a Christmas tree.

They're carried by a windy tide.
In every basket people ride.
Was it not meant for man to fly
Would God have given him the sky?

Pumpkin Song

Halloween pumpkins
Are mountains of gold,
Piled in the stores
When the weather grows cold,
Looking so lovely
That no one would guess
Cutting them open
Could make such a mess.

Song for an Indian Child

The God who gave my people life
Is All and yet is One—
The music of the pounding rain,
The heat behind the sun;

The deer that grazes on the hill,
The eagle overhead,
The thick, brown river flowing past,
The fire that bakes our bread.

In summer, corn springs from his hand,
In winter, drifts of snow.
He watched my people build these walls
A thousand years ago.

He goes not by a Christian name
But walks among us all the same.

Leaf Song

It's autumn, and the leaves grow old.
Their vibrant green turns rust and gold
And finally brown. The wind comes by
To soothe them with a lullaby.

They flutter to the song she sings
And drop like birds with heavy wings
To settle in a weary heap
And crackle once and fall asleep.

Song for Something Little

Thank you, Lord, for little things—
Tiny birds with untried wings,
Fuzzy kittens, butterflies,
Baby colts with solemn eyes.

We'll be gentle, Lord, and kind
To the little things we find,
Knowing once, when we were new,
We were very little too.

Song of Surprise

When the Lord used to speak
To the prophets of old
There was lightning and thunder,
Or so we are told.
How the mountains would shake
And the bushes take fire
When God roared from the skies
In a bellow of ire!

So I always supposed when
God's voice called to me
That's exactly the volume
I'd know it to be,
And I never suspected
I'd find it one day,
Stirring, soft, in my heart
In the gentlest way—

Like the wind in the trees,
Like a trickle of sand,
Like the brush of a bird
On the palm of my hand.

Song for Sisters

Sisters in the springtime,
Young, they were, and fair,
Sharing secret whisperings,
Ribbons in their hair.

Busy, golden summer
Drew their lives apart.
Distance has no meaning
For the loving heart.

Autumn came to meet them.
What has been has been.
Sisters are forever;
They are home again,

As the air grows sharper,
As the trees grow bare,
Sharing secret whisperings,
Silver in their hair.

Song of Thanksgiving

For food and drink and candlelight,
We thank you, Lord, this special night.
For loved ones who have gathered near,
For those we love who are not here,
For making us this world to share,
We bow our heads in grateful prayer.
With earthly joys so freely given,
What wonders may we find in heaven?

Parent Song

My mother and my father have
A life apart from me.
It's strange to think that they were here
Before I came to be,
That there were things they talked about
And things they found to do
To fill those dull and vacant days
When they were only two.

I'm glad to know that when I'm grown
They'll manage somehow on their own.

Song for Hanukkah

In winter when the days grow short
And dark falls thick and fast,
My people tell the story of
The Light That Could Not Last.
They tell of lifting high their lamp
And calling out God's name.
Jehovah heard their plaintive cry
And breathed upon the flame.

The darkened temple filled with light
As from the rising sun;
One single night's supply of oil
Burned seven days and one!

In winter when the skies hang low
And daylight hours are few,
We gather with the ones we love
And pledge our faith anew.
To celebrate God's gracious gift
Of never failing light,
The little fires of Hanukkah
Dance, joyful, in the night.

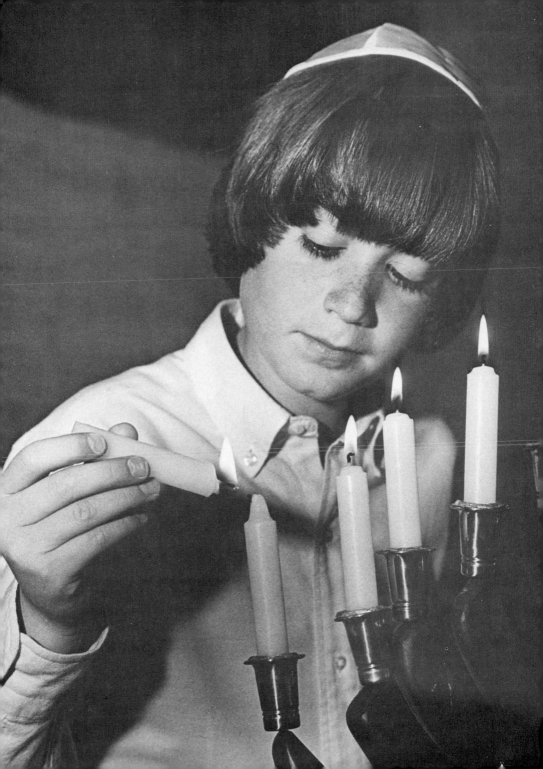

Song for Christmas Eve

There was a star that shone one night
And filled the world with crystal light.
The shepherds watching from afar
Looked up and wondered at the star.
The wise men, many miles away,
Beheld the star and thought it day.

How strange that one lone baby's birth
Could cause such light to flood the earth.

Mountain Song

Clouds form the hair of the mountains,
Piled in a snowy crown,
Tumbling over the shoulders,
Stooped and aged and brown.
Gnarled arms circle the forests.
Laps cup meadows and streams.
Here from the earth's beginning,
Dreaming inscrutable dreams,
Sometimes mountains look haggard,
Staring off into space;
Sometimes, touched with the sunset,
Soft as a grandma's face.

Song to Get Wet By

The Indoor People clean their rooms.
They vacuum well. They're good with brooms.
Their shoes are always polished bright.
They keep their buttons sewed on tight.
They visit with their parents' guests,
And study for their spelling tests.
Their English themes are never late,
And all their dresser drawers are straight.
They play guitars. They're well-trained cooks.
They read an awful lot of books
And always know the authors' names.
They're super great at video games.
Yes, Indoor People get things done.
(But Outdoor People have more fun.)

Song of Promise

What is springtime? Nothing now.
All the streams are frozen still.
Snow lies heavy on the land.
Nothing stirs upon the hill.

Branches stretch against the sky,
Bare and black and very old;
Trees that have forgotten spring
Shiver, silent, in the cold.

What is springtime? Nothing now.
Still, there is the faintest sound,
Whispering beneath the earth—
Laughter deep in frozen ground.

And so, the circle is complete.
The sun grows warm. The air grows sweet.
The seeds that sleep beneath the earth
Awaken, yawn, and then give birth
To tiny shoots that flower and grow
To burst in triumph through the snow.
Their many-colored melodies
Go rippling out upon the breeze.

God writes the songs that children sing
Throughout the year, from spring to spring—

Acknowledgments

The author owns the rights to all poems in this collection. The following were previously published:

ABBEY PRESS: "Wedding Song" in *Marriage and Family Living,* June 1977, copyright 1977 by Abbey Press. "Song for Christmas Eve" in *Marriage and Family Living,* Dec. 1980, © 1980 by Abbey Press.

THE CHURCH OF JESUS CHRIST OF LATTER-DAY SAINTS: "Balloon Song" in *The Friend,* June 1980, copyright 1980 by The Church of Jesus Christ of Latter-day Saints.

THE CURTIS PUBLISHING COMPANY: "Song for a Farm Child" in *The Saturday Evening Post,* Aug. 1954, © 1954 The Curtis Publishing Company.

ENCYCLOPAEDIA BRITANNICA EDUCATIONAL CORPORATION, from the program Language Experiences in Reading: "Moon Song" and "Song of Change," copyright 1975, "Song of Frustration," copyright 1974, by the Encyclopaedia Britannica Educational Corporation.

THE SUNDAY SCHOOL BOARD OF THE SOUTHERN BAPTIST CONVENTION: "Phone Song" in *Living with Teenagers,* July 1982, © 1982 The Sunday School Board of the Southern Baptist Convention. "Song for Something Little" in *Living with Preschoolers,* April 1980, © copyright 1980 The Sunday School Board of the Southern Baptist Convention. "Song of Promise" in *Mature Living,* Jan. 1981, © copyright 1980 The Sunday School Board of the Southern Baptist Convention. "Song of Wealth" in *Living with Teenagers,* July 1981, © copyright 1981 The Sunday School Board of the Southern Baptist Convention.

Index of First Lines

About the Author

LOIS DUNCAN started sending stories to magazines at age ten and sold her first story when she was thirteen. When she was twenty she wrote the first of her twenty-seven books. During her teens she wrote regularly for youth publications such as *Seventeen* and placed three times in their annual short-story contests.

She lives in Albuquerque, New Mexico, with her husband and five children. Photography is her hobby. She likes horseback riding, musical comedy, mystery novels, travel, and doing things with her family. She hates cold weather, housework, sweet potatoes, loud rock music, chewing gum, most forms of healthy exercise, and cleaning the oven!

The children in the photographs are Lois Duncan's own youngsters, her nieces and nephew, her children's friends and her friends' children, so it's sort of a family album. The gentleman on the front cover, being hugged by granddaughters, is the man to whom this book is dedicated —her father.